THE DIVINE
MERCY CHAPLET

A Deep Meditation

James Mark

THE DIVINE MERCY CHAPLET: A DEEP MEDITATION

This book is written to provide information and motivation to readers. Its purpose is not to render any type of psychological, legal, or professional advice of any kind. The content is the sole opinion and expression of the author, and not necessarily that of the publisher.

ISBN   978-1-64552-027-6   (Paperback)
ISBN   978-1-64552-028-3   (Digital)

Lettra Press books may be ordered through booksellers or by contacting:

Lettra Press LLC
18229 E 52nd Ave.
Denver City, CO 80249
1 303 586 1431 | info@lettrapress.com
www.lettrapress.com

Blanchette Catholic Center
16555 Weber Road
Crest Hill, Illinois 60403
Phone 815-221-6100
www.dioceseofjoliet.org

May 12, 2014

Mr. James Mark

Braidwood, Illinois 60406

Dear Mr. Mark:

The designated Diocesan censor has completed a review of the manuscript, *Divine Mercy Chaplet – A Deep Meditation*, by Mr. James Mark. I understand that Rev. John Balluff, S.T.D. communicated directly with you regarding various corrections and/or clarifications on the material. He otherwise found it to be in conformity with the teachings of the Church. Therefore, I am pleased to grant the *Permission to Publish* in accordance with the requirements of Canon 824 of the Code of Canon Law. The following text, in bold type, must be printed in the book:

Nihil Obstat	*Permission to Publish*
Reverend John Balluff, S.T.D.	**Most Reverend Joseph M. Siegel, D.D., S.T.L.**
Censor Deputatus	**Vicar General**
April 27, 2016	**Diocese of Joliet**
	May 12, 2016

The *Nihil Obstat* and *Permission to Publish* are official declarations that a book is free of doctrinal and moral error. No implication is contained therein that those who have granted the *Nihil Obstat* and *Permission to Publish* agree with the content, opinions, or statements expressed. Nor do they assume any legal responsibility associated with publication.

I would also like to point out that this approval is given for this version of the text *only*. Should you or your publisher make any further revision of the text (other than to implement the recommendations of the censor or to correct typographical errors) or if you wish to print a subsequent edition in which the original text is modified, you must seek the approval of the diocesan bishop of the place where the author currently resides or where the work is being published.

After publication, please send two copies of the work to Sister Judith Davies, OSF, Chancellor for the Diocese of Joliet, for filing in the Diocesan Archives.

Sincerely in Christ,

Most Reverend Joseph M. Siegel
Auxiliary Bishop and Vicar General
Diocese of Joliet

PREFACE TO THE BEGINNING OF THE DIVINE MERCY CHAPLET

Jesus, our Good Shepherd, during His sorrowful passion asks us not only to follow Him, but also asks us to walk with Him. He calls to us, " Little lambs, little lambs, don't run ahead of Me and don't lag behind Me. Just walk with Me." Hopefully, we will muster the courage to respond, "Yes, Lord, I will walk with You" and Jesus replies, "Then take My hand and walk with Me, keeping your eyes focused only on Me." By doing this we mere humans can console the heart of Jesus on His way to Calvary and the cross [1]

THE DIVINE MERCY CHAPLET A DEEP MEDITATION

Jesus says in the diary of St. Faustina, "There is more merit to one hour of meditation on My sorrowful passion than there is to a whole year of flagellation that draws blood; the contemplation of My painful wounds is of great profit to you and brings Me great joy."[1]

"When you pray this chaplet at the bed of a dying person I will stand as mediator of Divine Mercy and not as Just Judge. That person will die a peaceful death."[2]

Intention: Anyone you wish, examples are: someone you know who is sick, or someone who is dying or has died recently, people suffering from natural or man-made disasters, soldiers overseas, or for fallen away Christians or yourself and your family.

Directions

The regular Divine Mercy is a short prayer/pamphlet that can be said in about 10-15 minutes and can be said daily.

I would recommend saying this version about once a month to remind the reciter of the overwhelming love that Jesus has for us as He freely endures these sufferings during His passion and death in order to pay the price of our salvation and open up to us the the marvelous gift of heaven through His Divine Mercy.

It is my hope that the reading and occasional rereading of this Passion will aid you as you pray and meditate on the regular chaplet and the sorrowful mysteries of the rosary.

In A Group

In a large or small group, this may be prayed interactively. The standard text should be read by the leader. The bold text should be read by all the participants.

LET US BEGIN

In the name of the Father, and of the Son, of the Holy Spirit. Amen.

Opening prayer:(optional) You expired Jesus, but the source of life gushed forth for souls, and the Ocean of Mercy opened up for the whole world. O Fount of Life, unfathomable Divine Mercy, envelop the whole world and and empty Yourself out upon us. (Diary 1319)

Our Father, Who art in heaven, hallowed be Thy name; Thy kingdom come; Thy will be done on earth as it is in heaven. Give us this day our daily bread; and forgive us our trespasses, as we forgive those who trespass against us; and lead us not into temptation, but deliver us from evil. Amen.

Hail Mary, full of grace, The Lord is with you. Blessed are you among women, and blessed is the fruit of your womb, Jesus. Holy Mary, Mother of God, pray for us sinners, now, and at the hour of our death. Amen.

I believe in God, the Father Almighty, Creator of heaven and earth. I believe in Jesus Christ, His only Son, our Lord, who was conceived by the power of the Holy Spirit and born of the Virgin Mary. He suffered under Pontius Pilate, was crucified, died, and was buried. He descended to the dead. On the third day, He rose again. He ascended into heaven, and is seated at the right hand of God, the Father Almighty. From there, He will come again to judge the living and the dead.

I believe in the Holy Spirit, the holy Catholic Church, the communion of saints, the forgiveness of sins, the resurrection of the body, and life everlasting. Amen.

DECADE #1
THE AGONY IN THE GARDEN

Eternal Father, we offer You the body and blood, soul and divinity of Your dearly beloved Son, our Lord Jesus Christ...

In atonement for our sins and for those of the whole world.

1. Father, for the sake of His sorrowful Passion.... **Have mercy on us and on the whole world.**

   It is evening. Jesus, unknown to the eleven apostles, has just finished the divine love feast, their Last Supper together. The moon lights up the night with all of its full glory as the Jewish feast of Passover approaches. They are walking to the Garden of Olives to pray, and it is the day Jesus will die.[3]

2. For the sake of His sorrowful Passion.... **Have mercy on us and on the whole world.**

   They stop at the gate and eight of the apostles remain there. Jesus with Peter, James, and John, walks deeper into the garden saying, **"My soul is sorrowful even to death. Remain here and keep watch with me... Watch and pray that you may not undergo the test."**[4]

3. For the sake of His sorrowful Passion.... **Havemercy on us and on the whole world.**

    Jesus walks about a stone's throw away, collapses to his knees, then prostrates himself on the ground and prays, **"Abba(daddy), Father, all things are possible to You. Take this cup(of suffering) away from Me."**[5]

4. For the sake of His sorrowful Passion.... **Have mercy on us and on the whole world.**

    The Evil One comes and tempts Jesus, (possibly saying), "This is a waste. These humans are not worth Your trouble. In spite of what You suffer, they will still lust for pleasure, power, wealth, sex, and succumb to other addictions. They won't care. All You do and all Your pain will be for nothing."

5. For the sake of His sorrowful Passion.... **Have mercy on us and on the whole world.**

    Jesus gets up and goes back to the three apostles. He says to Peter and the others who have fallen asleep, **"...So you could not keep watch for one hour? Watch and pray that you may not undergo the test. The spirit is willing but the flesh is weak."**[6]

6. For the sake of His sorrowful Passion.... **Have mercy on us and on the whole world.**

As Jesus returns the devil again whispers in His ear, (possibly saying), " Peer forward into history, and observe how mankind obeys Your law of love: Hitler, Stalin, the Holocaust, ourselves, abortion on demand, pornography, the world wars, child abuse, and abuse of alcohol and drugs. It is just not worth Your pain, suffering, and death for this ungrateful race." Jesus is in such mental agony that His sweat turns to drops of blood

7. For the sake of His sorrowful Passion.... **Have mercy on us and on the whole world.**

An angel comes and comforts Him, (possibly saying), "Remember not the evil ones. Peer into the future to see those who do love You and do keep Your commandment of love–the martyrs and saints, Francis, Anthony, Catherine, Teresa, John Paul II, Bonhoffer, Gandhi, Martin Luther King, ourselves, and all the unnamed billions of priests, nuns, and lay people who devote their lives to believing in You, praising You, loving You, caring for the poor, as well as our own daily works, prayers, and sacrifices. All You endure allows them to follow You. They will take up their crosses and come after You. If just one comes to You, Your sacrifice will be worth it.

8. For the sake of His sorrowful Passion.... **Have mercy on us and on the whole world.**

Again Jesus prays," **Father, if You are willing, take this cup(of suffering) away from Me; still, not My will, but Yours be done.**"[7] And by His obedience, Jesus atones for Adam's disobedience.

3

9. For the sake of His sorrowful Passion.... **Have mercy on us and on the whole world.**

    Judas arrives with an entourage of soldiers to arrest Jesus. Judas approaches Him and kisses Him on the cheek saying, "Hail, Rabbi" **Jesus replies, "Judas, are you betraying the Son of Man with a kiss?"**[8] The soldiers arrest Jesus and march Him off to the high priest and the Sanhedrin for trial. (The Sanhedrin is the tribunal of Jewish priests and elders.)

10. For the sake of His sorrowful Passion.... **Have mercy on us and on the whole world.**

    On the way to trial they prod Him, beat Him, and curse Him over and over again. When they arrive at the Sanhedrin, they beat Him again, mock Him, and bring false witnesses against Him.

DECADE #2
THE SCOURGING

Eternal Father, we offer You the body and blood, soul and divinity of Your dearly beloved Son our Lord Jesus Christ.

In atonement for our sins and those of the whole world.

1. Father, for the sake of of His sorrowful Passion.... **Have mercy on us and on the whole world.**

   In the Sanhedrin, the members of the Jewish hierarchy having no believable witnesses illegally make Jesus testify against Himself. The high priest questions Him," Are you the Son of the living God?" Jesus answers, **"You say that I am."**[9] Caiaphas, the high priest, tears his garments and says, "What further need do we have for witnesses. You have heard the blasphemy." And so they condemn Him to death.

2. For the sake of His sorrowful Passion.... **Have mercy on us and on the whole world.**

   Meanwhile, as Jesus foretold just a few hours earlier, three times Peter denies that he knows Him. When the rooster crows the second time, Peter remembers Jesus' words and runs off weeping bitterly.

3. For the sake of His sorrowful Passion.... **Have mercy on us and on the whole world.**

Judas hangs himself ...Suicide-The ultimate rejection of trust in God and God's merciful love. Even after 3 years of living with Jesus, Judas can not trust in God's merciful forgiveness. When WE are truly sorry, WE cannot out-sin God's loving mercy.

4. For the sake of His sorrowful Passion.... **Have mercy on us and on the whole world.**

The Jews bring Jesus to Pilate, the Roman governor. Pilate sees their jealousy and tries to free Jesus. He allows the crowd to choose to release Barabbas, the murderer and insurrectionist, or Jesus, the King of the Jews.....They choose Barrabas.

5. For the sake of His sorrowful Passion.... **Have mercy on us and on the whole world.**

Pilate orders Jesus to be scourged, hoping the crowd will show mercy when they see His beaten and torn body.

6. For the sake of His sorrowful Passion.... **Have mercy on us and on the whole world.**

Jesus is whipped. The whip, called a flagrum, is made up of two leather straps tipped with tiny metal balls, shards of pottery, pieces of bone, or rusty nails. These rip into Jesus' tender flesh leaving his back with the appearance of raw hamburger when the soldiers finally stop.

7. For the sake of His sorrowful Passion.... **Have mercy on us and on the whole world.**

About 40 strokes with the Roman flagrum, could be enough to kill a man. Jewish law allowed only 39 strokes, but, as Isaiah foretold of God's Suffering Servant over 600 years ago, Jesus remains silent during the beating. The Roman soldiers go into a frenzy trying to make him cry out, whipping him about 60 times. (This is evident on the Shroud of Turin.)

8. For the sake of His sorrowful Passion.... **Have mercy on us and on the whole world.**

Each stroke of the flagrum creates an explosion of pain in the brain of Jesus-Whack/agony. Whack/ agony. Whack\agony, on and on 60 times. Each stroke endured is reparation to the Father for our sins against purity. His body is abused because we have abused ours. Finally, slipping in his own blood, Jesus is carried away from the pillar.

9. For the sake of His sorrowful Passion.... **Have mercy on us and on the whole world.**

Since the accusation against Jesus is that He is a king, The soldiers weave a crown of thorns in the form of a cap. They place a purrple cloak over the bloody wounds on His back, and in His hand and they place a reed to symbolize His scepter of office. They ram the cap of thorns onto His head, and beat Him about His head with the" scepter". In mocking veneration they genuflect before Him, saluting Him. and saying, "Hail King of the Jews." Then they blindfold Him, slap Him, spit on Him, and punch Him.

10. For the sake of His sorrowful Passion.... **Have mercy on us and on the whole world.**

Jesus is brought back before Pilate and Pilate says to the crowd, "Behold the man." So bloody and sore is He that we can hardly recognize Him as human. 600 years before His birth, Isaiah prophesied about Jesus this way: "He was spurned and avoided by men, a man of suffering, knowing pain, like one from whom you would turn your face...But it was our pain that he bore; our sufferings He endured. We thought Him as stricken, struck down by God and afflicted, but He was pierced for our sins, crushed for our iniquities... and by His stripes we are healed."[10]

DECADE #3
JESUS IS CONDEMNED TO DEATH

Eternal Father, we offer You the body and blood, soul and divinity of Your dearly beloved Son, our Lord Jesus Christ.

In atonement for our sins and for those of the whole world.

1. Father, for the sake of His sorrowful Passion.... **Have mercy on us and on the whole world.**

    Pilate announces, "I find no guilt in this man." But the chief priests and Pharisees persuade the crowd to call out for His crucifixion, "Crucify Him! Crucify Him!"

2. For the sake of His sorrowful Passion.... **Have mercy on us and on the whole world.**

    "Why? What evil has He done?" Pilate asks, "What shall I do with Jesus, your King?

3. For the sake of His sorrowful Passion.... **Have mercy on us and on the whole world.**

    "We have no king but Caesar. Crucify Him! Crucify Him! Crucify Him!"

4. For the sake of His sorrowful Passion.... Have mercy on us and on the whole world.

Pilate is scared–a riot is brewing; but Jesus has done no wrong–What to do? What to do?

5. For the sake of His sorrowful Passion.... Have mercy on us and on the whole world.

Fearing a riot, Pilate ceremoniously sits down and washes his hands in front of the crowd announcing, "I am innocent of the blood of this just man. Crucify Him yourselves." But is Pilate really innocent?

6. For the sake of His sorrowful Passion.... Have mercy on us and on the whole world.

Pilate turns Jesus over to his soldiers again. They present Him with the cross. He embraces it. It is the horizontal beam weighing about 125 pounds. They place the heavy burden on the raw wounds on His shoulders, and tie His arms outstretched to the beam. His knees buckle, and He almost falls as Jesus begins the long road to Calvary.

7. For the sake of His sorrowful Passion.... **Have mercy on us and on the whole world.**

After walking a short distance, His foot catches in the cobblestone road. He reels trying to catch Himself, but with His arms tied outstretched to the beam He cannot protect Himself as He falls face down into the muck and the dung on the road.

8. For the sake of His sorrowful Passion.... **Have mercy on us and on the whole world.**

   Jesus struggles to His feet. He is extremely weak and pale. But He recognizes someone in the crowd. Someone who has been weeping. He sees His mother, Mary, who has such sorrow written on her face that it wrenches Him to His core. He groans, **Oh, Mama!**

9. For the sake of His sorrowful Passion.... **Have mercy on us and on the whole world.**

   Mary elbows her way through the crowd. Finally, their eyes meet in a silent communion of their love and sorrow – God's two most perfect human beings are paying the price for our salvation.

10. For the sake of His sorrowful Passion.... **Have mercy on us and on the whole world.**

    A sword of sorrow tears through Mary's Immaculate Heart and soul- just as Simeon had foretold 33 years ago when she presented Jesus in the Temple 40 days after His birth.

DECADE #4
THE LONELY ROAD TO CALVARY

Eternal Father, we offer You the body and the blood, soul and divinity of Your dearly beloved Son, our Lord Jesus Christ.

In atonement for our sins and those of the whole world.

1. Father, for the sake of His sorrowful Passion....**Have mercy on us and on the whole world.**

    The soldiers shove Mary out of the way to examine Jesus. He must not die on this journey to the Skull place. He is weak and his eyes are glassy, but He is not about to die... just yet. They untie the beam removng the heavy burden from His damaged shoulders.

2. For the sake of His sorrowful Passion.... **Have mercy on us and on the whole world.**

    A large burly the man in the crowd is pressed into service replacing Jesus under the heavy beam. Simon of Cyrene reluctantly begins to carry the weighty load.

3. For the sake of His sorrowful Passion.... **Have mercy on us and on the whole world.**

    Ah! Some relief! The anxious soldiers smile and nod at each other. Jesus may survive to Calvary after all. The crucifixion will go on!

4. For the sake of His sorrowful Passion.... **Have mercy on us and on the whole world.**

What's happening? Again there's a disruption in the crowd. A young woman forces her way through the unruly crowd and pushes her way to Jesus. Veronica takes the cloth she carries and gently wipes His face.

5. For the sake of His sorrowful Passion.... **Have mercy on us and on the whole world.**

Jesus leaves the imprint of His bloodied face on her cloth. The Roman soldiers shove her back into the crowd.

6. For the sake of His sorrowful Passion....**Have mercy on us and on the whole world.**

Jesus, weakened from loss of blood, beatings, and unremitting pain, forces in one foot in front of the other, moving toward the ultimate goals of His life – His death and resurrection. In spite of the removal of the cross beam, He falls twice more. Then He ministers to some weeping women at the side of the road, **"Daughters of Jerusalem, do not weep for Me; weep instead for yourselves and for your children..."**[11]

7. For the sake of His sorrowful Passion.... **Have mercy on us and on the whole world.**

At last, Jesus, exhausted, hungry, thirsty, mangled, and bloody, arrives at Golgotha. They strip Him of His garments, ripping open the wounds of is scourging again. And He stands before all debased, bleeding, and naked.

8. For the sake of His sorrowful Passion....**Have mercy on us and on the whole world.**

The soldiers beckon Jesus to lie down on the cross beam, now attached to the cross. As He lies down they pull His right arm towards the end of the beam, grab a huge nail, and pound it into His wrist. Bam! Bam! Bam! An explosion of pain washes over His brain as His thumb involuntarily closes into the palm of His hand.

9. For the sake of His sorrowful Passion.... **Have mercy on us and on the whole world.**

Next, the soldiers violently wrench His left arm toward the opposite end of the beam. The nail. Bam! Bam! Bam! The explosion of pain. The thumb closes. Jesus' silent scream pierces the air.

10. For the sake of His sorrowful Passion.... **Have mercy on us and on the whole world.**

The executioners then nail His feet to the cross. Again as the cruel nail pierces each foot, Jesus undergoes unimaginable agony as the unstoppable pain rushes through His brain.

DECADE #5
THE DEATH OF JESUS

Eternal Father, I offer You the body and blood, soul and divinity of Your dearly beloved Son, our Lord Jesus Christ.

In atonement for our sins and for those of the whole world.

1. Father, for the sake of His sorrowful Passion.... **Have mercy on us and on the whole world.**

   After the executioners raise Jesus, crucified on His cross, He calls for forgiveness, just as He had taught so often before, **"Father, forgive them for they know not what they do."**[12] He prays for His executioners, His enemies, and for us!

2. For the sake of His sorrowful Passion.... **Have mercy on us and on the whole world.**

   After the cross is raised, Jesus realizes He can't breathe. His body screams for air. Suddenly, almost automatically, His legs begin pushing on the nail piercing His feet. As He rises, stress is removed from His ribcage and His lungs can contract and expand; but only while He keeps pressure on the nail in His feet. When He becomes too tired or the pain becomes too great, His body sinks down. His ribcage becomes paralyzed again and His body screams for air once more. For at least three hours, He repeats this agonizing ritual before He dies for us.

19

3. For the sake of His sorrowful Passion.... **Have mercy on us and on the whole world.**

"Amen, I say to you, today day you will be with me in Paradise."[13] He promises heaven to the repentant Good Thief, the first person of the New Covenant to enjoy the benefits of salvation through His Divine Mercy. His Mercy is available to all even at the brink of death! Just repent and ask!

4. For the sake of His sorrowful Passion.... **Have mercy on us and on the whole world.**

Then Jesus, looking at John standing under the cross, speaks to Mary, His mother, **"Woman, behold your son."**[14] Then He says to John the Apostle, as our representative, **"Behold your mother."**[15] Jesus gives us all that He has, including His own mother.

(Perhaps, He calls her "Woman" to show that Mary is the Woman promised at near the beginning of Genesis, after Adam's sin, whose offspring will crush the head of the evil serpent from the Garden of Eden. Here we witness the fulfillment of God's first promise to the human race.)

5. For the sake of His sorrowful Passion.... **Have mercy on us and on the whole world.**

Jesus cries out **"I thirst."**[16] He thirsts not only for water, but He also thirsts for our souls. The soldiers give Him vinegar to drink.

6. For the sake of His sorrowful Passion.... **Have mercy on us and on the whole world.**

Then He raises Himself up and with His hard-won breath calls out, **"My God, My God, why have You abandoned Me?"**[17] Is Jesus despairing, giving up on God's mercy and love?

No! He begins to recite Psalm 22 written by David 1000 years before Jesus was born, describing precisely what He is presently enduring: "I am a worm, not a man, scorned by men...All who see me mock me, they shake their heads at me...Like water my life drains away...My tongue cleaves to my palate...They have pierced my hands and feet; I can count all my bones...but You, Lord, My strength, come quickly to help Me."

7. For the sake of His sorrowful Passion.... **Have mercy on us and on the whole world.**

"It is finished"[17] With the most extreme effort Jesus raises Himself and says these words with which He opens the gates of heaven to all the saints of the Old Testament and to us. Jesus reconciles us with the Father paying the price of our salvation in full.

8. For the sake of His sorrowful Passion.... **Have mercy on us and on the whole world.**

Jesus sinks back down. Then He painfully rises up and, with His final breath, announces His death, **"Father, into Your hands I commend My spirit."**[18] He bows his head and dies.

9. For the sake of His sorrowful Passion.... **Have mercy on us and on the whole world.**

Some time after this uterance, the Roman centurion in charge has to make sure that Jesus is truly dead. He skillfully thrusts his lance through His ribs and into His heart. Immediately, blood and water gush forth from the wound. The battle-hardened soldier attests "Truly, this man was the Son of God."

10. For the sake of His sorrowful Passion.... **Have mercy on us and on the whole world.**

Oh, Blood and Water, which gushed forth from the Heart of Jesus, as a fountain of Mercy for us, I trust in You.

Oh, Blood and Water, which gushed forth from the heart of Jesus, as a fountain of Mercy for us, I trust in in You.

Oh, Blood and Water, which gushed forth from the heart of Jesus, as a fountain of Mercy for us, I trust in in You.

Holy God, Holy mighty One, Holy Immortal One, Have Mercy on us and on the whole world.

Holy God, Holy mighty One, Holy Immortal One, Have Mercy on us and on the whole world.

Holy God, Holy mighty One, Holy Immortal One, Have Mercy on us and on the whole world.

Optional Closing Prayer: Eternal God, in Whom Mercy is endless and the treasury of compassion inexhaustible, look kindly upon us and increase Your Mercy towards us, that in difficult moments we might not despair nor become despondent, but with great confidence, submit ourselves to Your most holy will, which is Love and Mercy itself.

ALLEULIA ! ALLEULIA!

ON THE THIRD DAY REJOICE BE GLAD! HE IS RISEN! HE IS RISEN! HE IS RISEN

ALLEUIA

JESUS, I TRUST IN YOU

THE SUFFERING PRAYER

by Bill Scheer Immaculate Conception Parish
Braidwood, Illinois

O Jesus, I know that suffering comes to all of us at various times in our lives-for some more than others. Let me accept my suffering today whether physical, emotional, or spiritual, as it allows me to participate in Your plan for the redemption of the world. Let my suffering unite with Your suffering, death, and resurrection as it works to call sinners back to Your Sacred Heart and to the love that You have for each of us as Your brothers and sisters.

O Jesus, let me not sink into despair as I face my suffering today, but rather let me turn to You for comfort and courage. Jesus, I know that You love me far more deeply than even I know. Help me to be courageous as I face my suffering this day- knowing that You are with me at every moment. Let my suffering be a gift that I give to You this day. It is my prayer of repentance and thanksgiving that I offer to You in reparation for my sins and in thanksgiving for all the blessings that You have showered upon me. And especially, I ask that You use it for those who are lost and far from Your love. Call them back to Your loving arms, Lord. Thank You, Jesus for calling me to participate with You in Your mission. I love You, Lord Jesus! Help me to love You more each day. Amen.

ENDNOTES

1. Diary of St. Faustina paragraph 369.

2. Diary of St. Faustina paragraph 1541.

3. In Israel, even today, their next day begins at sundown. For example, after sundown on Friday, Saturday begins and since it is the Sabbath almost all economic and government activity cease. In Genesis as God creates the universe each new day begins in the evening: "Evening came and morning followed the (number) day."

4. Mark 14:36 NAB

5. Mark 14:37-39 NAB

6. Luke 22:42 NAB

7. Luke 22:48 NAB 42

8. The Day Christ Died by Jim Bishop 1977. Published by Galahad books 1993. p.382.

9. Luke 22:70 NAB

10. "A Doctor at Calvary" by Pierre Barbet, M.D., 1953 p 83.

11. Isaiah 53:3-5 NAB

12. Luke 23:28 NAB

13. Luke 23:34 NAB

14. Luke 23:42-43 NAB

15. John 19:26-27 NAB

16. John 19: 28-29 NAB

17. John 19: 30 NAB

18. Mark 15:33-34 NAB

19. John 19:30 NABRE

20. Luke 23:46 NABRE

21. Mark 15:39 NABRE